"I Have

Cheese

Doodles

Up My Nose!"

Quotes from an Elementary
School
Nurse's Office

By Carol Kasper, RN

Kasper Publishing
70 Old Farm Road
East Longmeadow, MA 01028

First Edition

ISBN 978-1-9804-3100-8

For the children
And those who care for
them

I Have Cheese Doodles Up My Nose!

For twelve years, I had the opportunity to work as the school nurse at an elementary school with children from the ages of 3 to 8. I say work, but many days I just thought of it as going to school to be with the children. I knew that no matter how busy, or frustrating, or sad, the day ahead might turn out to be, I would find a smile and usually a laugh within that day.

Children, as we all know, are fiercely honest. Talking with the school nurse affords a certain intimacy and the comments are often even more surprising in their frankness.

Here I present these comments written just as I heard them. I hope you will gain a smile, perhaps a laugh, and an appreciation for the wonder of childhood.

C.K.
2018

I Have Cheese Doodles Up My Nose!

Table of Contents

I Have Cheese Doodles Up My Nose!

Comments are offered
on
A Variety oF SubjectS-

I just had my
birthday – I was five
years old forever!

Last week I was stung by a killer bee.

We are going to Elvis' house, even though he's dead.

I figured out my math problem. I used my fourteen fingers!

I accidentally had an accident.

My teacher says I go to the nurse a little bit a lot.

⌘

I need to take a rest– my mom keeps waking me up in the morning for school!

 *ZZZzzz*

I am in a really bad mood today, so I need to go home.

This is the tenhundreth and eightieth time I've gotten hurt.

My dad thinks it's the chicken pops.

My cousin had her independix out.

I am going to the doctor today for the bump on my leg—it's sillyitis!

MedICaL coNcerNS

are very difficult to describe when you are very young- - -

Child walking into nurse's office from recess: I think I broke my back.

Child with laryngitis:

My voice is low.

After eating a spicy meal:

My heart hurts.

The doctor said I had cracks in my lungs.

I need some gasoline for my lips.

I don't know why, but when I run in the heat, I get hot.

My head is steaming!

I feel like there is a tack in my hair.

I have struck throat.

I need my lips chapped.

My cough started when I was born.

C★C★C★

My stomach is hurting because I was breathing too much.

()

When I eat my soup, I feel like poop!

When asking child how he felt when he was absent:

I felt like a bird with a shot wing.

My nose is bleeding- and I wasn't even picking it!

I know I'm breathing, but I feel like I'm not.

My friend put gloop in my ear.

I Have Cheese Doodles Up My Nose!

CONVErSatioNS

can be difficult---

Child: I got scratched by a pricker bush.

Nurse: Where did you get scratched?

Child: Outside.

Nurse: Where did the bush scratch you?

Child: When I was running.

Nurse: Where on your body did the bush scratch you?

Child: Oh, on my hand.

Child: I'm bleeding!
Nurse: Where?
Child: Right here at school.

Nurse: Who is your teacher?

Child: (Looking confused) She's in my room.

Child: I just went to Disney.
Nurse: You did? When?
Child: The day after tomorrow.

I Have Cheese Doodles Up My Nose!

NaMeS are very Hard
for a small child—

Nurse: What is your last name?

Child: Junior.

Nurse: Your last name is Junior?

Child: Yes, John James Thomas Junior.

My name is Emily Elizabeth Smith but you can call me Emily Smith.

Nurse: What is your name?

Child: Will.

Nurse: What's your last name?

Child: (long pause) Yum.

My dog's first name is Rusty– I don't know his real last name.

Explanations can be
A Marathon Sport-

I almost caught the football and then it went in the mud and I did too.

I have good news and bad news—I lost my tooth! But then I swallowed it.

My friend bumped into me and my tooth came out and I was so happy I hugged her!

Imissmymommy
Imissmydaddyschool's
too
longmylegsgettiredI
feelsickandIwannago
home!!

I can't tie my shoe cuz there's a knot in it and I can't get the knot out cuz my nails are too short and my nails are too short cuz I bite them.

Child coming with a bump to his head:

I ran into the wall. I guess I should have walked.

When you are 6 years old, there are so many
MedicaL MySteries-

Yesterday my cough was medium, now it's triple power!

My temperature was 99 and I was throwing up. When it's 100 you must be dead.

It feels like a pin is going into my head every now and then.

My head is hot and my brain hurts.

It feels like a train is going through my head.

My mommy thinks I have an ear confection.

A friend describing the illness:
He thinks he has a beaver.

My red is nosey.

You hear things said by
CoNFUSed adULtS
you will not hear anywhere else—

You wait until the bathroom door is shut to pull down your pants.

No cartwheels in the hall, please!

He came out of the bathroom with his underwear in his hands.

! !

I Have Cheese Doodles Up My Nose!

EXpLaNatioNS May deFy LoGic—

Flying fruit hit my eye.

👓 👓 👓

A penguin's beak got me.

I only know how to tie my shoes at home.

I Have Cheese Doodles Up My Nose!

ASK a StUPid qUeStioN...

And well, you know---

Nurse: Do you want me to take out your splinter?

Child: (When sees tweezers) Oh, it's just a freckle!

Nurse: What room are you in?
Child: The playground.

Child: I need some bandaids for my classroom.

(Nurse, hoping to hear the word *please*, places her hand to her ear.)

Child: I NEED SOME BANDAIDS FOR MY CLASSROOM!

Child: My dad is a doctor.

Nurse: Oh really, what kind?

Child: The kind that takes care of sick people.

Nurse to First Grader: Is your hair itchy?

Child: My hair has been itchy since Kindergarten!

Nurse: What grade are you in?

Child: I'm not in a grade– I'm in kindergarten.

Nurse: What is your last name?

Child: (looking unsure)

Um, my whole family has it!

Child: My allergies keep me chewing.
Nurse: Chewing?
Child: You know– achooing!

Other

PitHy obSerVatioNS:

When treating a child's abrasion during the first week of school:

I don't care if it stings, cuz ... now I'm in the second grade!

I know how to spell
your name–
J-A-K-UP!

After noticing some blood
to a little girl's nostril–
I don't pick it. I'm
a lady!

After stepping on a tack the previous week and then sitting on a tack that day:

I have a problem with tacks.

Child remarking on his cut:

It's like when my dad got a bloody finger from cutting squash. That night I got to have pizza!

7 year old on his scrape:

I've had much worse. I suppose my birth was much worse.

When I grow up I'm going to be Santa Claus.

6 year old after losing a tooth:

I've been waiting my whole life for this!

7 year old relating a story:

That happened a hundred years ago when I was just a kid.

My teacher says I'm a hard cookie!

⌘

Oh no, I broke the law! My mom said not to come to the nurse anymore.

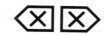

My tooth fell out- it means I'm growing up.

I feel a little pukey today.

I'm not brave when I get a shot 'cuz I'm six years old!

When I play in the rain, I get wet.

I'm a great first grader. I've practiced for years!

At the zoo we're going to see a spider monkey.
I don't know if it's half spider or half monkey.

This is the threeist time I came here.

During hand washing lesson:

Nurse: When is it a good time to wash your hands?
Child: After you pick your nose.

On my birthday, I will be 6, the next year 7, and it keeps on going 'til you're dead.

☠☹☠

I'm going to my nana's– her backyard is like a dumpster!

My mommy loves me.
Mommies are for love.

♥ ♥ ♥

Acknowledgements

I wish to thank my family for their love and encouragement to complete this project.

I also wish to thank the children and staff at Meadow Brook Elementary School for the insightful comments made during my 12 years as their school nurse.

It was my privilege to spend each day with their ready smiles and open hearts.

CK

I Have Cheese Doodles Up My Nose!

I Have Cheese Doodles Up My Nose!

I Have Cheese Doodles Up My Nose!

I Have Cheese Doodles Up My Nose!

Made in the USA
Lexington, KY
17 July 2018